God's Worried

Satirical
verse by
Roger Woddis
from the New Statesman

Introduced by James Cameron
Illustrated by John Minnion

© *Roger Woddis*

Typeset and printed by
Manchester Free Press
59 Whitworth St, Manchester 1
061-228 0976

Published by
New Statesman, 10 Great Turnstile, London WC1

ISBN 0 900962 15 1

Trade distribution by
Scottish & Northern Book Distributors Ltd,
18 Granby Row, Manchester 1

&

48A Hamilton Place, Edinburgh EH3 5AX

Southern Distribution
Albion Yard, 17A Balfe Street, London N1

Cover & illustrations: John Minnion

For you.

Introduction
James Cameron

AS A TITLE "God's Worried" is all very well, and doubtless only too true, but there is another more recondite anagram of the Bard's name, revealed to me in a dream.

"Ower Gorsidd" is well known to all good Welshmen (and there are one or two) as the resident spirit of the foothills around Greath Turnsthial, an elusive yet persistent organism inhabiting the grey midlands of New Statesmanland, giving pleasure to the righteous (or more properly the lefteous) and dismay to the Establishment prigs and pricks in places high and low, and above all middle.

Go forth, brave Gorsidd, and keep on worrying God.

I like writing forewords for Roger's books; to be assembled within the same cover is like sharing a taxi with Swift. He is—almost alone today—in the direct tradition of the great eighteenth century satirists. His weekly verse in the NS is usually, though not always, a parody. Parody lends itself to delicate cruelty; to turn a Victorian sentimentality into a contemporary shaft of acid is a most satisfying way of achieving two things at once.

It is not practical to select from the Woddisiana any lines that synthesise the character of the *oeuvre,* if I may call it that (he will be parodying me next, you wait) each verse belongs to the moment, and its message needs that moment to be complete. Roger is a journalist, albeit twenty times more able than most of us—wittier, defter, more skilfully bitter. To be simultaneously sardonic and sentimental is the unique Gorsiddian gift.

When you and I were young, lad, and all the skies were blue, politics were Stan and Clem, to name but one or two. You couldn't really hate them; they were not even funny; to write at all about them you had to need the money.

Time passed and brought us Ted and Jim, and who remembers them? Then Downing Street went into drag, and wished us Mrs M...

Envoi. Hail to the king of the carpers and naggers. He gives one good reason for buying the Staggers.

A double Sulphuric, and pass me his glass, to get in the mood for a kick up the backside.

Stand aside, Gorsidd, we have your number.

Who Did For Dutschke?

Who did for Dutschke?
'I', said the Lawyer,
'With terminer and oyer,
I did for Dutschke.'

Who got him framed?
'I', said the Spy,
'With my little lie,
I got him framed.'

Who tapped his phone?
'I', said the Copper,
'Tapped it good and proper,
I tapped his phone.'

Who called him names?
'I', said the Peer,
'In my *Daily Smear,*
I called him names.'

Who sent him packing?
'I', said the Minister,
Looking slightly sinister,
'I sent him packing.'

And morale everywhere
Was given a boost—
Till the birds of the air
Came home to roost.

15 January 1971

A Policeman's Pay

With acknowledgements to W.S. Gilbert

(Police representatives have turned down a two-stage pay offer of an immediate 10 per cent increase, with an additional offer later.—News item.)

When a copper's not content with his employment,
He can't come out on strike or work to rule.
When the evening crowds are seeking their enjoyment,
He is usually out a-working like a mule;
If he isn't dealing with a demonstration,
He is searching rooms for pot or solving crimes,
So to publicise his lot, the Federation
Has placed a half-page advert in *The Times.*
When you think of how he labours day and night,
A policeman's income isn't worth a light.

What with prices and the cost of living rising,
They're putting in for 35 per cent;
On their present pay it's hardly so surprising
That most are broke, and some are slightly bent.
You would think from certain programmes on the telly
That a policeman's duties drive him up the wall,
But so far from pounding suspects to a jelly,
He dearly loves the public—'Evenin', all.'
When constabulary forces join the race,
Their claim, no doubt, will prove a 'special case'.

18 December 1970

Toujours la Politesse

*(In a reprimand to the North Vietnamese
delegate to the Paris peace talks for
allegedly insulting President Nixon,
Mr David Bruce, chief American delegate,
said: 'At least one should be courteous if
one cannot be quiet.')*

Our function in a world beset
By strife and tension is to teach
The basic rules of etiquette
Correcting every tasteless breach.

The Vietnamese have yet to learn
Diplomacy's a solemn rite;
It's not bad form to maim or burn,
The crime is not to be polite.

If, in some minor incident,
The death of children should occur,
A brief note after the event,
Tinged with regret, is *de rigueur.*

Never belittle or revile
The fellow on the other side,
And always wear a winning smile
When spraying crops with herbicide.

If enemies, to shift the blame,
Should cast you in the villain's role,
Bow and continue with the game
Of international protocol.

This above all: though blood is spilt
Avoid all words that give offence,
And wear, no matter what the guilt,
A look of injured innocence.

13 November 1970

Market Quadrille

(Acknowledgements to Lewis Carroll)

'Will you come into the Market?' said the President of France,
'There's a purpose in my asking, and it's made me
                                    change my stance.
See how cunningly the Germans have produced their box of tricks!
They are waiting to take over—will you come and join the Six?
Will you, won't you, will you, won't you, will you join the Six?
Will you, won't you, will you, won't you, *won't* you join the Six?'

'You can really have no notion how disastrous it will be
If the mark continues floating and the franc's thrown out to sea!'
And the PM said he couldn't wait to mingle with the Six—
He was wholly hooked on Europe and was dying for a fix.
Would not, could not, would not, could not live without a fix.
Would not, could not, would not, could not live without a fix.

'The trouble is the Commonwealth is breathing down my neck,
But I'll pay the price you ask for—will you take a rubber cheque?'
'*Attendez!*' cried the President, 'before you count your chicks,
You must ditch New Zealand farmers if you want to join the Six.
Will you, won't you, will you, won't you, will you join the Six?
Will you, won't you, will you, won't you, won't you join the Six?'

'As soon as one door closes,' giggled Heath, 'another shuts.
We must move towards agreement, though we hate
                                    each other's guts.
I could still the voice of conscience if it wasn't for the pricks
And the loss of Tory votes when I surrender to the Six!
Shall I, shan't I, shall I, shan't I, shall I join the Six?
This year, next year, sometime, never, *ever* join the Six?'

21 May 1971

Margaret's Song

*'The savings to be effected by changes in
the arrangement for school milk amounted
to £5.9m. this year, but £9m. in a full year.'
—Mrs Margaret Thatcher, 14 June.*

Take, O take that milk away
That so freely was doled out;
Osteomalacia
Causes less concern than gout:
Children who are really ill
Only have to read my Bill.

Put away that handkerchief,
Millions will be saved a year:
Think of all the tax relief
Given to the profiteer.
Thus we help the needy few,
As we promised we would do.

Local councils who intend
Making breaches in the law
Would be criminals to spend
More than is provided for—
Woe betide them if they dare
Pouring pintas everywhere!

Take, O take that milk away,
Never mind parental moans;
Future generations may
Have bad teeth and softened bones,
But they'll find tomorrow sweet,
Standing on their malformed feet.

18 June 1971

Teddy Heath's Picnic

*('...some part of the price inflation that is now so much of a bad
dream to so many ordinary people can be blamed directly
on the policies of the present Government...'*
—Financial Times, *8 June)*

If you go down to the shops today,
You'll probably do your nut;
If you go down to the shops today,
It's better to be half-cut,
For everything you see on the shelf
In price has damn near doubled itself,
'Cos that's the way you pay for Teddy Heath's Picnic.

Picnic time for Teddy Heath,
The lot he represents are having a lovely time today;
When he smiles and shows his teeth,
You simply have to turn your head away,
See him laughing like a clown,
He'd bring those prices down,
He said, at a single stroke:
It's nice to know a handful of teddies
Are doing rather well,
Though the rest of the country's broke.

11 June 1971

Bicentenary
Robert Owen, 1771-1858

'This was a man whose ancestors might well have included an elf or a fairy, to whom he owed his talent for making money like magic and spending it all on dreams.'—Viscount Eccles, House of Lords, 5 May. 'In spite of the fact that he spent large sums of money upon schools, houses and playing fields, his mills at New Lanark showed an ever-growing balance on the right side. He made huge profits.'—Lord Maelor.

If only we knew how he did it!
If we could but borrow his spell
For coming by money like magic,
What fabulous stories we'd tell
Of loyal, contented employees
And multiple profits as well!

> *And did those hands in ancient time*
> *Laws of the country contravene?*
> *And was the holy Bill of Carr*
> *In Robert Owen's England seen?*

The founders of cooperation
Believed in the goodness of man,
But sharing the nation's resources
Is hardly a practical plan,
When life is much less than a love-match
And more of a catch-as-catch-can.

> *And did Cupidity Divine*
> *Lay waste our wealth and human skills?*
> *And were the unions gelded there*
> *Among those bright New Lanark mills?*

Our laws against juvenile labour
Exploited for minimal pay
Owe much to the Owenite theory
That children should come out to play,
Though many were thereby deprived of
The joys of a fifteen-hour day.

Bring me a weary ten-year-old!
Bring me a paper-boy to hire!
Bring me my Mail! O Times, unfold!
Bring me my early-morning quire!

Though clearly a model employer,
And morally sound his crusade,
The vision he had of Utopia
Is only a dream, we're afraid:
A lavishly stocked cornucopia
Would upset our balance of trade.

We cannot set the world aright
By building castles in the sand,
Nor hope to build Jerusalem
In England's port-and-pheasant land.

14 May 1971

Prisoners

*'It is difficult to see what the North Vietnamese
hope to gain from their systematic breaches of
the Geneva Convention on prisoners of war,'*
—Bernard Levin* in The Times, *29 April.*

When Levin's fulgurating mind
Is turned on Vietnam,
Demanding captors should unbind
The sacrificial lamb;
When we lie tangled in his prose
And dazzled by his name,
We marvel that he dare expose
The propaganda game.

When many come to fight the few
With planes and guns and tanks,
The least the Vietnamese can do
Is offer up their thanks;
When airmen have done all they could
To bomb their country flat,
Apparently the peasants should
Write 'Welcome' on the mat.

Soft hearts do not an army make,
Nor charity a shell,
And there are harder things to take
Than in a prison cell;
If tears must flow for pilots' wives,
How many must we shed
To mourn a million crippled lives
And half a million dead?

*levin, n. lighting.—dictionary definition.)

7 May 1971

Nixon's Song

(Acknowledgements to Ray Noble)

The very thought of Mao
And I forget somehow
Those little revolutionary things
That everyone's quoting now;
I need a cure for my depression,
My hopes are on Peking,
And if it ends recession,
To me that's everything.

Though peace is long delayed,
There's yearning here for trade,
You'll never know
How low
The profits go
Till a deal is made;
I'm longing for a game of ping-pong,
A smile from Chou En-lai,
But most of all right now
I'm hoping Chairman Mao
Will buy.

23 April 1971

Second Reading

('The word government had used for people having the right of abode was "patrial". It was not the best of words. Its great advantage was that it made it possible to get away in the Bill from the term "alien", which he had always disliked.'
—Maudling, reported in The Times.*)*

Come into the open, Maud,
For the black cat's in the road,
Come, admit your Bill's a fraud,
For it's written in secret code,
With its figleaf phrases designed to conceal
And its bogus 'right of abode'.

There had risen a rousing cheer
From non-patrials at the gate,
They thought they'd be coming here
And be able to serve the state;
But the Monday Club cried, 'No fear!'
And the Liberals wept, 'Too late!'
And a backbencher woke and mumbled 'Hear, hear,'
And a Powellite hissed, 'I hate.'

And whether the Bill means fewer
Or more with a darker skin,
And whether they'll feel secure,
Once Maudling has let them in,
One thing is certain sure,
The champions of kith and kin
And those who claim their motives are pure
Are brothers under the skin.

12 March 1971

The Old Multiracial

(Mr Vance Dickie, Victoria's State Minister for Immigration, has confirmed in a BBC radio interview that Australian policy on immigration could be described as 'racialist'.)

Once a jolly spokesman sat down in Victoria,
Under the shade of a colour-bar tree,
And he sang as he sat and eulogised the Commonwealth:
'Don't come the old multiracial with me.'

Old multiracial, old multiracial,
Don't come the old multiracial with me,
And he sang as he sat and eulogised the Commonwealth:
'Don't come the old multiracial with me.'

Down came a non-European British citizen;
Up jumped the spokesman and spilt all his tea.
And he sang as he talked of white assisted passages:
'Don't come the old multiracial with me.'

Old multiracial, etc.

So sang the spokesman to that coloured immigrant,
'You'll never get me to change,' said he,
And his cry may be heard at the break-up of the Commonwealth:
'Don't come the old multiracial with me.'

Old multiracial, etc.

22 January 1971

Hang the Whale!

Let the savage whale be slaughtered,
Hung, garrotted, drawn and quartered,
And its carcase cut to pieces
As a warning to the rest!
Back the Japanese and Russians,
Down with blubbering discussions,
For the so-called threatened species
Is an anti-social pest!

Scott is just too bloody gentle,
Spike is soft and sentimental:
Who is goon and who knight-errant?
Kill the terror of the deep!
Drag him crying through the shallows,
Let him die upon the gallows,
Use the ultimate deterrent
While the wildlife weirdos weep!

Why accuse us of despoiling,
When our motor-cars need oiling?
Save the consecrated dipstick,
Guard the gear-box that we love!
Think of starving hordes in Asia
Needing protein from Cetacea,
Not to speak of ladies' lipstick
And the softened leather glove!

20 July 1979

Joke over

Pravda *has called on Soviet comedians to make 'a deep analysis of current events' as the basis for witty monologues.*

It was Chortle Day in the Kremlin,
And Brezhnev told his staff:
'Enough of current problems,
It's time we had a laugh.
I've got this stand-up comic—
No, quiet, please, don't shout.
You've read your *Pravda,* comrade—
Now make us fall about!,

The comic made up stories
From items in the news,
Of clothes that fell to pieces,
And drunks and leaky shoes;
And wheat that was imported—
'It goes against the grain'—
And soon the Politburo
Was laughing like a drain.

'There was this workers' leader,
Whose name began with B;
He had a country *dacha*
And a villa by the sea...'
And when the joke was finished,
A heavy silence fell.
He now has two kind doctors,
And drugs to make him well.

10 August 1979

Force of argument

The BBC has agreed to submit details of programmes to the Metropolitan Police when these cover 'delicate' police areas.

This is the bold Corporation,
Voice of the more-or-less free,
Where producers talk to head people,
And the heads to Sir David McNee.

Five years ahead lies the vision,
Big Brother watching the slave.
'Only the Thought Police mattered'—
But Orwell is dead in his grave.

Delicate subjects are dicey,
Not, heaven help us, taboo;
It's just that one has to be servile
When putting an opposite view.

The problem in making a programme—
Or one that is going to be seen—
Is licking the hand on your shoulder,
While keeping one eye on the screen.

In totalitarian countries,
Where banning's the name of the game,
The ground-rules are totally different—
Well, anyway, not quite the same.

The price that we pay for our freedom
Is not being quick on the draw,
But being eternally watchful
(And especially watching the law).

15 June 1979

The senator's prayer

Bless our hawks, O Lord, we pray,
Lest we sign our arms away;
Let our ironware increase,
Guard us from the threat of peace.
Give us strength to call a halt.
Season not our tears with salt;
Though the Treaty ink has dried,
Let it not be ratified.

Let salvation still be found
In a silo underground;
Keep the missiles we possess
Programmed and in readiness
Let all talk of mutual trust
Crumble to atomic dust,
And the course of world affairs
Boost our military shares.

Save our souls, or, if you like,
Send us a pre-emptive strike;
Let not radicals destroy
Half the weapons we deploy.
Lead us not towards detente,
One last blessing you can grant:
If you are the Power above,
Shoot down, Lord, that goddam dove.

18 May 1979

On duty bent

'There seems to be a correlation between such persons (joggers) and homosexual nuisances.'—A police field manual.

While proceeding down the High Street,
Ruminating on my lot,
I observed the prisoner running
At a fairly steady trot.
He was wearing satin gym-shorts,
With his hair done up in bows,
And I came to the conclusion
That he must be one of those.

There was lewdness in his movements,
There was make-up on his face,
So I took hold of my truncheon
And immediately gave chase.
I pursued him past the tailor's
And the ironmonger's shop,
Till I caught him by the cobblers,
Thus compelling him to stop.

I then said I'd be appearing
As a witness for the Crown,
And I warned him any statement
Would at once be taken down.
But he shook his fist and shouted,
'Oh, don't be a silly sod—
Can't you see I'm from the Special
Anti-Homosexual Squad?

31 August 1979

Love Song

A former headmaster in Moffat,
Dumfriesshire said after being cleared of
assaulting boys: 'I love being a
prep-school head and put my heart and
soul into it.'

My love is like a red, red weal
That's raised on tender skin:
My love is like a riding-crop
That whips my charges in.

As keen art thou, my bonnie cane,
So strong of arm am I;
And I will use my manly strength
Till I have made them cry:

Till I have made them cry, my dear,
And had my harmless fun:
And I will be within the law,
And the law will say, 'Well done'.

Till they are meek and disciplined,
I shall not spare the rod,
And I will beat their buttocks blue,
And put my trust in God.

And though my calling is in vain,
And some may call it vile,
I thank the Lord I have the cane
To make it all worthwhile.

5 October 1979

Blood on the tea

A report by the World Development Movement claims that British tea companies are continuing, despite recent pledges, to exploit tea pickers.

I'm shocked and disgusted
To think that I trusted
The Co-op and Brooke Bond
To lighten their toil.
The charge is plain-spoken:
The promise is broken,
There's blood on the tea,
And my own's on the boil.

It pains me to say it,
The way they portray it,
The picture is one
That I'd rather not see.
The companies were lying,
The young are still dying;
I'm sick when I think
Of the profits from tea.

What use are petitions
To end these conditions?
The firms should be fined,
And the shareholders shot.
It's all so upsetting,
I'm shaking and sweating—
Oh, is there another one
Left in the pot?

9 November 1979

White carpet

Welcome to Britain
From sunny South Africa!
Know, Mr Botha, how warmly we feel.
That goes for both of us—
I am Lord Carrington.
This fellow? Oh, he's the Lord Privy Seal.

How are you, Prime—?
Silly me!—*Foreign* Minister.
(Very confusing, your names both the same).
Let's see, you're 'Pik'—
Am I right?—he's P.W.—
Sad about Muldergate, no-one's to blame.

Lovely to have you,
And how is Pretoria?
What can we do for you, now that you're here?
Put on a Press gag
To deal with unpleasantness?
Make a few dangerous types disappear?

Look how the crowds
Are all waving to welcome you.
What have they got on their banners? Let's see:
'Go home, you hangman'—
A term of endearment.
We do have a droll sense of humour.
More tea?

22 June 1979

Ship of state

*The Chancellor, Sir Geoffrey Howe,
said in an interview in the* Wall Street
Journal *that the British economy is 'off
course'.*

The outlook, I fear,
Is appallingly bad:
The engine is failing,
The captain is mad.
We've long lost our bearings,
We're drifting off course;
We'd signal for help,
But we never learnt Morse.

The compass is broken,
The wheel is askew,
We'll know where we're bound
If we ever heave to.
The crew is a rabble
Of mutinous dogs,
And we'd write it all down
If we understood logs.

The first mate's half-crazed
With a terrible tic,
The doctor is drunk
And the engineer's sick.
We're listing to starboard,
The radio's dead,
So let her go sideways—
And full steam ahead!

24 August 1979

Scousefrau

The Memoirs of Bridget Hitler edited by
Michael Unger Duckworth £4.95

How thorny is the parth they tread
Who try to disinter the dead,
And how beset by traps the sleuth
Determined to unearth the truth.
Some readers may believe this book
Deserves a long and trusting look,
While others, sceptic to a fault,
Will take it with a pinch of salt.

It seems there was a Dublin Miss
Who met and married Alois,
Half-brother to the man who later
Became the not-so-great Dictator.
Her name was Bridget Dowling (née),
Until her fateful wedding-day,
When life, that clown in cap and bells,
Inspired the story that she tells.

Her memoirs, published now in full,
Describe those months in Liverpool,
Where Adolf Hitler, not so daft,
Had journeyed to escape the draft.
In 1912, despite the rain,
They met him off the Lime Street train,
An apt case for an analyst.
He nearly drove them round the twist;
He lay in bed for half the day,
Until, when he'd outlived his stay,
His brother, who could stand no more,
Exclaimed, *'Mein Gott,* you're twenty-four!
Why don't you leave, or take a job?
Get out and graft, you lazy slob!'
But Adolf, showing scant concern,
Replied, 'I first must English learn.'

In 1913 Adolf left
For Munich, and his hosts, bereft
Of sanity and near despair,
Were more than glad to pay his fare.
What follows—Bridget tells it all
With total and undimmed recall—
Includes a loving son called Pat,
Who sometimes knew what he was at;
A foreign tour (she sang, you see)
With Harry Lauder's company;
But central to this masterpiece
Is Adolf's fondness for his niece,
A girl called Geli who, it seems,
Awoke his love and filled his dreams.
Alas, the girl was shot and died,
A case of so-called suicide,
Though Bridget thinks there's little doubt
That Uncle Adolf rubbed her out.

We learn of Hitler's little quirks:
His passion for detective works,
His faith in what the stars foretell,
The way he ate his food as well,
His love of films and German dogs—
All this and more she catalogues.
He thought (the evidence is slim)
That every woman fancied him.

All this may be a load of bull,
But Bridget broods on Liverpool.
A question preys upon her mind:
She asks herself, 'If I'd been kind,
Would Adolf's plans have come to naught?'
What, no Third Reich? Now there's a thought.

4 May 1979

A slight amendment

The National Association of Schoolmasters/
Union of Women Teachers conference at
Eastbourne agreed to delete the word
'passionate' from a motion on corporal
punishment.

This conference now reaffirms—
let us be careful of our terms—
its passionate—um, ardent?—view—
no, neither of those words will do.
Of course, we want to keep the cane
but after all we *are* humane,
and therefore we should not exalt
our love of legalised assault.

No, what we really need's a phrase
that sounds restrained and yet conveys
why some—nay, most,—of us are bent
on using corporal punishment.
So passion's out—but how about
'Our right to give a kid a clout
is on occasion justified,
and may include infanticide.'

You murmur? You do not approve?
Then this perhaps—'We hereby move
that smarting seats and broken skin
are normal forms of discipline,
and beating them with lengths of wood
not only does the children good,
but also wonders for our glands.'
Will those in favour raise their hands?

27 April 1979

Par for the Course

'The radiation level is what people would get if they played golf in the sunshine.'—A spokesman for the U.S. Nuclear Regulatory Commission.

And after the game in the golden sunshine,
After we'd come to the eighteenth hole,
We wondered about these goddam burn-marks,
And Chuck said to treat them with alcohol.

Laughing and lurching, we reached the clubhouse,
Harry was hoarse with a lousy cough,
And aiming to prove I could hold my liquor,
I tried to stand up and my leg fell off.

Eddie made noises and sorta bubbled.
Harry said, 'Fellows, I'm feeling sick.'
Chuck was explaining how golf was harmless,
When Eddie turned blue and began to tick.

Then Harry threw up and said, 'I'm poisoned',
And I turned away from his melting face.
'What is your handicap, Chuck?' He answered,
'I guess it is being a cancer case.'

After the game in the molten sunshine,
They switched off the 'phone at the NRC.
The ghosts playing golf now on Three Mile Island
Are Harry and Eddie and Chuck and me.

6 April 1979

Stuff To Give The Troops

*'In the last few years Labour have fed and
nourished the worst instincts in the trade
union movement.'—Mrs Thatcher.*

How doth her iron ladyship
Reprove trade union power,
And wallop little bees who sip
The honey from the flower!

How grandly doth she strike a pose!
How holier-than-thou!
How soundly she belabours those
With sweat upon their brow!

Could we but imitate her class,
And give up what we hold,
Then none of us would value brass,
And all be good as gold.

The winter of our discontent
Will never change to spring,
While we go on about the rent,
And every other thing.

How rarely would we pour the wine
And wear expensive furs,
If all our instincts were as fine
And spiritual as hers!

30 March 1979

Sympathy

'Things change so terribly fast these days. Look at the Shah of Iran, poor man.'—The Queen Mother.

If only seasons never altered,
If only things remained the same,
If only roses bloomed forever
    And moths survived the flame!

I weep into my sleepless pillow
To see the Peacock overthrown,
And feel his tragic loss as keenly
    As if it were my own.

If only reeds were never broken,
If only time and tide stood still!
I pray the worst may never happen,
    But rather fear it will.

If only we could be quite certain
The rest of us were here to stay!
The fear of change perplexes monarchs,
    As Milton used to say.

But while his plight evokes our pity,
We should at least give heartfelt thanks
That something salvaged from the wreckage
    Is safe in foreign banks.

And I for one shall count my blessings,
And close my ears to distant drums,
While there is yet a special fortune
    That smiles on Royal mums.

23 March 1979

Credo

'I believe in the people.'—Mr Callaghan.

I believe in our leaders,
The gangsters with tear-filled eyes,
Who think we are all half-stupid,
And cannot tell truth from lies,
The honey-tongued presenters
With clipboards between their thighs.

I believe in the talkers
Who've never produced a car,
The righteous who talk of mercy
And say we have gone too far,
Who plead for the sick and dying,
And know where the cameras are.

I believe in a saviour,
A blonde with a blue rosette,
The pygmies who can't remember,
The giants who can't forget.
I believe in the sleepers,
Who have not woken yet.

16 February 1979

All Clear

Nobody put their hand out,
Nobody took a bribe,
Nobody was compromised
By acts you could describe.

Nobody got away with it,
Nobody thought they could,
And all of them were honest men,
And all of them were good.

Nobody bought a silver gift
To please somebody's wife,
Nobody did a single thing
To poison public life.

Nobody bought a cabinet,
Whatever you may hear,
And all of them were honest men,
And all were in the clear.

Nobody did a secret deal,
Nobody was for sale,
Nobody bent the rules at all,
And nobody went to jail.

And all of them were honest men,
As white as driven snow,
And all lived on a higher plane,
And shat on those below.

9 February 1979

New Ramps for Old

China is restoring wealth and property to former millionaires.

With Deng all things are possible,
And Peking points the way:
Here is a thought to borrow,
Goodbye to present sorrow,
If we should do tomorrow
What China does today.

Consider how the clouds would lift,
How raging seas would part,
If we embraced our betters,
If banks forgave their debtors,
And in our fringe theatres
We saw a change of art.

There'd be a metamorphosis
In all we have and hold,
If all those called were chosen,
John Tyndall's name were Rosen,
And, wages being frozen,
Bill Rodgers felt the cold.

The guiltless would see justice done,
If judges doffed their wigs:
No bureaucrat would shove us,
Our enemies would love us,
And all the skies above us
Be dark with flying pigs.

2 February 1979

What is right

*'It can be a pitiless weapon, and against this pitilessness Christians must protest.'
—The Archbishop of Canterbury,
Dr Donald Coggan.*

Those who labour should be humble,
Workers should be workmanlike;
It is sometimes right to grumble,
It is always wrong to strike.

Marvel, brothers, when the Primate
Makes the shallow seem profound,
One eye on the current climate,
One ear to the middle ground.

Hear a voice expressing pity
For the helpless and the old,
Somewhat muted if the City
Should exert a stranglehold.

Damning strikers as destroyers,
Men of conscience must protest—
Keeping in with your employers
Dulce et decorum est.

He who crawls upon his belly
Serves the nation as a whole;
He who says, 'Not on your nelly'
Loses his eternal soul.

19 January 1979

An Honourable Man

The man his masters most revere
Is Herbert Swarf, the engineer,
Who rose from lathe to desk, whereat
He served the proletariat.
Determined from his earliest youth
To fight for Liberty and Truth,
He laboured long and soon became
A full-time keeper of the flame,
Who thought no staunch trade unionist
Should figure in an Honours List—
Until he heard the Royal Sword
Was poised to render him a Lord.

The dream he carried in his head,
Which seemed to some the deepest red,
Turned orange, thence to pink, then yellow:
Our Herbert had begun to mellow,
A process that, in place of strife,
Held promise of a quiet life.
His principles, already frayed,
Could not resist an accolade;
For, as he argued, 'Why refuse?
Deep down I've never changed the views
I've nurtured since I was a lad.'
Deep down, in fact, he never had.

5 January 1979

Bloody nurses

'With the reduced working week, the deal is equivalent to 20 per cent.'
—*the* Sun.
'This should add fat supplements to the nurses' pay packets.'
—*the* Guardian.

O wicked, selfish Florence,
Unmoved by human need!
We vomit with abhorrence
And shudder at your greed.
You bear a lighter onus
Than that of Doctor Fell,
And now you claim, as bonus,
A living wage as well.

Your pay-rise will enrich you,
Your work has been cut down;
You're hardly fit, you bitch, you,
To kiss the surgeon's gown.
The grievances you're nursing
Are no excuse to quit;
No saint needs reimbursing
For being in the shit.

Your posture is more ghastly
Than flesh and blood can stand;
The remedy is lastly
And lovingly to hand:
Angels can add benignly
To better pay than Clegg's
By lying down supinely
And opening their legs.

6 June 1980

Nerves, 1980

(After 'Nerves—2 September 1939' by
'Sagittarius')

I think I'll get a paper.
I think I'll break a date;
I think I'll have an early night,
I think I'll stay out late.

It's like the Cuban missiles
In 1962.
I can't think why I'm shaking.
Perhaps it's just the 'flu.

I couldn't eat a morsel.
I think I'll cook some grub.
I feel like getting good and pissed,
I can't afford the pub.

They're moving the Olympics
To Mablethorpe-on-Sea.
The Russians are in Pakistan,
It doesn't bother me.

I think I'll take a shower.
I'd better pay some bills.
I can't decide between the box
And taking to the hills.

No point in being nervous,
The nation's standing fast.
Suppose there is another war,
It's sure to be the last.

25 January 1980

Our man in Chile

*Britain is to exchange ambassadors with Chile.
Nicholas Ridley, junior Foreign Office Minister,
doubts whether Dr Sheila Cassidy was tortured by
Chilean secret police in 1975.*

The time was ripe, the signs propitious,
We did not have to ponder long,
Although we knew that rentachorus
Would very likely make a song.

The doctor did not get the treatment.
Electrodes? They were not applied.
The proof is clear beyond a shadow,
The accusation is denied.

Condemning Pinochet is caddish;
He seems a decent sort of chap,
Who stands for discipline and order,
And does not wear a greasy cap.

We shudder at the thought of torture,
Repressive systems we detest—
Unless, of course, their rugged methods
Defend the values of the West.

We have a sturdy friend in Chile,
We share, in essence, common aims,
So why not normalise relations—
Or Santiago for the Games?

There may be some who call us arseholes,
And others who object to this,
But after all, there's no denying,
We *are* the Foreign Orifice.

15 February 1980

Mine's a laager

'South Africa cannot afford the luxury of apartheid in sport and the Immorality Act while the Marxist bear is at our door.'—P.W. Botha, South African Prime Minister.

How brave is P.W. Botha,
How wise are his words and how just,
And after the recent disaster,
How blessedly swift to adjust!

The races stand shoulder to shoulder
Against the bad news from the North;
Now pass the dark days of unreason,
And something or other shines forth.

Let's talk of a new constitution,
Inviting the tame to take part,
That all the wide world in its wonder
May cheer at the change in our heart.

Let's build an acceptable future
For Coloureds, Mixed Races and Blacks,
And show we have changed our position
By shifting our seat on their backs.

We cannot afford old illusions,
We have to face facts as they are;
God smites us for doing too little,
God knows if we're going too far.

Though some may remain at their wagons,
And others may shudder to share,
The bite of the African lion
Is worse than the hug of the bear.

14 March 1980

Shoulder to shoulder

Proposals for constitutional reform

Talking Tough

'It would be tragic if the Thatcher Government fell a victim to Tory faint-hearts.'—Paul Johnson, in the Daily Telegraph.

If you can plunge in deep when other punters
Are taking damn good care to hedge their bets,
If you can flay the party's Billy Bunters,
And brand them all as wishy-washy wets;
If you can rant and not be tired by ranting,
Or when it comes to cuts, don't deal in pence,
Or being breathless, don't give way to panting,
And yet don't look too calm, nor talk much sense:
If you can wave your arms and get excited,
Or play with words—nor baulk at talking tough,
If you can wish your fellows were united,
But be too blind to see they've had enough;
If you can kill the crop and blame the seedman,
If you can praise the blight and cry 'Well done!',
Yours is the Earth laid waste by Milton Friedman,
And—which is more—you'll be a Lord, old son!

28 March 1980

Arms of the law

'A truncheon is a flimsy thing.' —Inspector Douglas Hopkins, head of
Scotland Yard's No. 3 Special Patrol Group.

Your actual copper's truncheon
Is a rather flimsy thing,
It couldn't split a human skull
Or break a vase of Ming.
It may be good for winding wool
Or propping up a milking-stool,
But when you've had a bellyful
Your rubber cosh is king.

Some use a pick-axe handle
Or a hosepipe filled with lead,
And a jemmy's pretty useful
For applying to the head;
But if you're bent on making meat
Of demonstrators in the street,
A rubber cosh is hard to beat
For stopping people dead.

23 May 1980

The Monetarist Samaritan

'No one would have remembered the Good Samaritan
if he only had good intentions. He had money as well.'
Mrs Thatcher, interviewed in Weekend World.

And a man going down to Jericho
Fell among thieves one day,
Who laughingly did him over,
And laughingly rode away.

And a holy priest and a Levite
Passed by on the other side,
Until there came a Samaritan,
Hard-headed and narrow-eyed:

Who said, 'I shall only assist thee,
And pour on the oil and the wine,
If thou suffered these wounds while working,
And not on the picket-line.'

And he told the man in his mercy
To stand on his own two feet,
And he counted out two denarii,
And asked for a stamped receipt.

And the poor man told the Samaritan,
'Put thy money back in thy purse:
Being robbed is a bad enough fortune,
Being preached at is even worse.'

11 January 1980

Safe as houses

'There is not the slightest danger, nor should anyone suggest it, of triggering off some kind of war by mistake.'—Defence Secretary Francis Pym.

Oh good, oh jolly good, I *am*
Relieved.
For one scary moment—
Well, two actually—or rather, three,
Including that hiccup last November—
I really believed
I'd be spread like jam,
Unfit to grace the human race,
Of which I am a paid-up member.

God, when I think
How the papers said
For three whole minutes
We were on the brink!
I blame the media.
They blow everything up,
Make things look worse than they really are.
It's far from *finita,* the old *commèdia.*
There'll be no war.

Well, I know next time.
When they talk of terror
And tell me I'm for it
Because of some small error
Curving through the sky,
I shall just ignore it.

13 June 1980

Persons represented

*Conservative MPs Teddy Taylor and Eldon
Griffiths have attacked the use of an Arts
Council grant in staging* A Short Sharp Shock,
which lampoons the Government.

The purpose of a public grant
To companies producing plays
Is not to shock a maiden aunt
Or have her bursting from her stays,
But to provide the kind of shows
For people sitting in the stalls
That help them to a sweet repose
And do not boast of having balls.

No one objects to poking fun,
The sceptred race can take a joke;
It all depends on how it's done,
But more, at what and whom you poke.
Theatre can be gay or grave,
The ancient mask is double-faced:
The dissident abroad is brave,
At home he shows the worst of taste.

A Dane of former times has shown
How drama can so score a hit
That guilty creatures have been known
To scream and jump about a bit.
The Leader has replaced the King,
But Claudius still fears the Prince;
As once before, the play's the thing,
And nothing much has altered since.

27 June 1980

Hand me a hairshirt

'Unemployment is to a certain extent self-inflicted.'—Industry Secretary Sir Keith Joseph.

I am a wicked worker
(Or was until last week);
I plot the country's downfall,
And know whereof I speak.

The wind that shakes the barley,
The germ that rots the bone,
All natural disasters
Are my design alone.

If I could shun the union
And break my hoops of steel,
I'd learn to love my masters
And kiss the iron heel.

If I were patriotic
And less consumed with greed,
I wouldn't put my children
Before the City's need.

I'd never go to Ascot
Or wallow in champagne,
If I were less besotted
With self-inflicted pain.

But now I've seen my folly,
I shall repair the wrong
By building here in Britain
The heaven of Hong Kong.

4 July 1980

Sermon in Brazil

*The Pope told a meeting of Brazilian
industrialists and businessmen that if social
justice were withheld, it would be achieved
'by the forces of violence.'*

Blessed are the poor in spirit,
for theirs is the quick way to heaven.

Blessed are they that live in luxury,
for they shall be comforted.

Blesed are the meek,
for they shall see where it gets them.

Blessed are they that hunger,
for they shall be fed with words.

Blessed are the powerful,
for they shall keep their power.

Blessed are the pure in heart,
for they shall believe anything.

Blessed are the speechmakers,
for they shall be called wonderful.

Blessed are they that are tortured,
for they shall gain humility.

Blessed is the Church of the Poor,
for it shall say nothing
of the violence of the rich.

17 July 1980

Ode to joy

'You might say that we are following the Beethoven approach to weapons systems planning...finding a good theme and hitting it over and over again.'—William J. Perry, US Under-Secretary of Defence for Research and Engineering.

Joy, thou lovely bride of power,
Married to the Pentagon,
Thou shalt still survive the hour
When the rest are dead and gone!
Thine is not to comfort others
Asking for their daily bread;
All shall call upon their mothers,
Where thy cruising wings are spread!

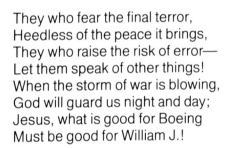

WHEN I HEAR THINGS LIKE **THAT** I'M GLAD I'M DEAF

They who fear the final terror,
Heedless of the peace it brings,
They who raise the risk of error—
Let them speak of other things!
When the storm of war is blowing,
God will guard us night and day;
Jesus, what is good for Boeing
Must be good for William J.!

Joy, thou lovely spark of gladness,
Lighting up the sullen earth,
Moving sober men to madness,
Bringing brighter worlds to birth!
He who seeks to end confusion
Finds his rest in thy embrace;
He who lives in self-delusion
Dies with egg upon his face!

18 July 1980

The only language

'People want peace so much that one of these days
governments had better get out of their way and let them
have it.'—President Eisenhower, 31 August 1959.

Ike, you should be living at this hour.
Moral pressures make protesters happy
But move few mountains. Words of passion
Are swallowed in the winds of power.

Rulers vary but are alike in this:
They do not listen or cringe before clamour.
Babies in prams, feet, voices
Are less than one stopping and unstoppable act.

Even as the placard is being painted,
Someone somewhere before a lighted screen
Sits with poised finger, awaiting orders.
Their precise calculations do not include reason.

The good delude themselves as well as others,
Their quiet cause the cue for distant laughter.
How many divisions has sincerity?
Liars and madmen are terribly sincere.

'Deter', they say, 'and you will live.'
It is the only language they understand.
If terror works, we should embrace their logic
And let our masters know what terror means.

22 August 1980

The Sundiposh

'Without weaponry, and facing a regime with no lack of it, they have been able to mobilise the yearning of ordinary working people for a measure of control over the circumstances of their lives.'
—Sunday Times.

A fabulous beast is the Sundiposh,
Regarded with awe by his peers;
His head is an inch from his rectum
And his testicles hang by his ears.
He screws up his eyes looking westward,
He opens them wide to the east—
In short and in all that he utters,
A most paradoxical beast.

His fear-call is 'Down-with-the-strikers!'
His nightmare is workers' control,
Unless it's Gdansk or Silesia,
In which case he cries 'Up-the-Pole!'
He crosses his legs in a crisis
And looks to the left for a spell,
To show he's not just double-jointed
But has double-vision as well.

He feathers his nest with old rubbish,
His sense of direction is sparse;
He soars in diminishing circles
And flies with his beak up his arse.
So always be kind to the Sundiposh,
In favour of unions abroad,
Applauding the power of the people,
But frankly, a bit of a fraud.

5 September 1980

Do not drop

*US Defence Secretary Harold Brown said there
was 'no destruction of the nuclear warhead, no
release of radiation material and no loss of security'
as a result of the Titan II missile accident at
Damascus, Arkansas.*

Everything's fine and dandy in Damascus,
They've swept up what remains of Titan II.
   A spanner in the works
   Can only frighten jerks
Who fail to see such accidents
Are really nothing new.

Nobody needs to fret about our warheads,
Nine megatons don't worry Harold Brown.
   He knows a minor scare
   Is neither here nor there;
We've got to keep pretences up,
Whatever else falls down.

Nothing can cause disaster in Damascus,
The comfort of the Bible sets us right:
   As Saul of Tarsus strode
   Along that famous road,
   He saw a flash from heaven
   That made his mind explode.
The rest of us would maybe sleep at night,
If Brown could be converted
By a sudden flash of light.

28 September 1980

Over the top

'The time has come when you had better stick your
heads up and come over the parapet.'
Mrs Shirley Williams.

'Twas shirlig, and the burkey notes
Did wax and wimble in the labe:
All flimsy were the borrowquotes,
And the modcons outfabe.

'Beware of the Labourleft, my son!
The laws that bite, the plots that hatch!
Beware the Grabgrab bird, and shun
The bennious Powersnatch!'

She took her gaitscal sword in hand:
With rage the evil foe she fought—
So waffled she for the Gang of Three,
And hardly paused for thought.

And as in rightish mood she stood,
The Labourleft, with eyes of flame,
Came marxing through the wedgy wood,
And chortled as it came.

One, two! One, two! The feathers flew,
While Liblabs praised her girlish guts:
The Slaveypress cried, *'Quelle noblesse!'*
And did their tiny nuts.

'And hast thou slain the Labourleft?
Come to our arms, our dreamish girl!'
'Let's hope and pray—but who can say?'
Replied the hapless Shirl.

3 October 1980

Cowboys

'Republicans have a habit of spreading around a lot of horse manure just before an election.'
—President Carter.

Oh, give me a home
Near the Capitol Dome,
Where a born-again Christian can pray;
Where seldom is heard
A Republican turd,
And the air has a lovely bouquet.

Home, home once again,
Where I'm sure as hell aimin' to stay;
Where hearts will be stirred
When I'm booted and spurred,
And I ride into town on the day.

Oh, let me stay pure
And untouched by manure,
Or the sound of it hitting the fan;
Though the fire has gone cold,
And the dream is on hold,
I still bank on a deal with Iran.

Home, home once again,
Where the donkey and elephant play;
Where I am preferred,
And the diff'rence is blurred
In the good old American way.

31 October 1980

Best Foot Forward

'An unmitigated folly.'—The Times *on the Labour Party leadership election result.*

When reckless Labour stoops to folly,
And causes decent chaps to pray,
What balm can soothe our melancholy,
What words explain it all away?

A leftward lurch induces terror,
And threatens values we conserve;
If such a choice was not in error,
It indicates a loss of nerve.

A sailor loth to prove his mettle,
Who pales to hear the timber split,
Does not expect the ship to settle,
And shows his faith by leaving it.

An energetic Opposition
Should always be our first concern,
But such an untoward decision
Gives tender souls a nasty turn.

The sight of all our hopes negated
Wrings bitter tears from every eye;
A barking dog must feel frustrated
To see the caravan roll by.

14 November 1980

Childish voices

A school hymn about public spending on war research has been condemned by the chairman of Dover Young Conservatives as 'introducing politics into schools through the back door.'

All things bright and beautiful,
All creatures great and small,
All dim Young Conservatives,
The Lord God made them all.

Each little clueless Tory,
Each nana who complains,
He made their childish voices,
He made their tiny brains:

The bomb that makes you bankrupt,
The germ that makes you die,
The flash before the fireball
That brightens up the sky:

The sub that rapes a city,
The ultra-phallic gun,
The missiles in their silos,
He made them every one:

He gave us heads of sawdust,
And lips that we might drool
How wicked is assembly
At Dover Grammar School:

All expensive armaments,
All profits great and small,
All things for the rubbish-heap,
The Lord God made them all.

21 November 1980

Open and shut

The BBC has cancelled a lecture on nuclear arms by Professor Michael Pintz, dean of science at the Open University, on the grounds that it was 'inappropriate and unsuitable'.

I am the very model of a safe Director-Gineral,
The water coursing through my veins is very largely mineral;
The way my powers are exercised, though more or
                                          less inscrutable,
Denotes an awful fear of things I deem to be unsuitable;
In controversial matters I display a certain latitude,
Except where the Establishment requires a kneeling attitude,
And while allowing programmes which are slightly
                                          on the bluey side,
I cannot think it wise to question universal suicide.

I draw the line at dissidents in matters academical,
Believing it disturbing to indulge in the polemical;
And if, instead of blessing war, a scientist should curse it, he
Will find the door is bolted at the Open University.

12 December 1980

Thanksgiving

Howe, do I love thee? Let me count the ways.
I love thee for thy heart and mind and soul,
Thy deep concern for those who are not whole,
The limbless eking out their crippled days.
I love thee for thy overflowing trays,
Dampened by tears for millions on the dole.
I love thee humbly for my begging-bowl;
I love thee for thy quiet disdain of praise.
I love thee with the passion of the old,
Whose bare existence is an act of faith.
I love thee with a love a thousandfold
More robbed of reason than a dying breath.
I love thee for my life—and, being cold,
I'll look to thee to answer for my death.

28 November 1980

Due for demolition

*The Conservative Party conference passed a
motion urging the strengthening of the House of
Lords as a safeguard against a 'Marxist state'.*

Lord Monday from his earliest years
Was keen to sit among his peers,
Though loth, of course, to take his pay,
Which came to umpteen pounds a day.
While not elected, he felt sure
His office was no sinecure,
And carried out his tasks with zeal
To guard, he said, the commonweal.

Imagine, then, his horror when
A former peer, now known as Benn,
Proposed, with fierce and fiery eyes,
To sever all our feudal ties
By pulling down the House of Lords,
Which plainly was a step towards
The building of a Marxist state,
With severed heads on every gate.

Lord Monday's voice was loud and clear:
'This threatens all we hold most dear!
An Upper House is vital to
The well-brought-up and well-to-do.
Without the Lords, and all its frills,
Who would there be to block the bills?'

Lord Monday tore his hair and cried:
The last I heard, he'd gone inside.

10 October 1980

One man's meat

'One man's pay increase is another man's place in the dole-queue.'—Sir Terence Beckett, director-general of the Confederation of British Industry.

One man's meat is another man's poison,
One man's gain is another man's loss,
One man's work is another man's torture,
One man's berk is another man's boss.

Jewels glow on the tongues of great ones,
Shining bright in the manner of lead.
'One man's rise is another man's dole-queue'
Makes good sense like a hole in the head.

Slashing pay will increase our markets,
Sounding off is the name of the game.
What they're told in competitor countries,
Strange to say, is precisely the same.

Money saved on a claim rejected
Goes to succour the crippled and weak:
See Sir T. shelling out his surplus,
Floods of tears down his sensitive cheek.

One man's meat is another man's poison,
One man's death is another man's health,
One man's love is another man's labour,
One man's freeze is another man's wealth.

3 July 1981

To Charliana of the faerie land

A Gentle Prince was trying on his geare,
Assisted by a hoste of loyal handes,
The whyles he mused on Dutie and Careere,
Which Breeding had established in his glandes:
He deemed his Realm the happiest of landes,
And happy his Emanuelled bride-to-be,
For both were pictured on a thousand brandes,
From silver ornaments to tinnes of tea,
Designed eftsoones to heal a sick economie.

So came they both in honore and displaye
To where the hush'd and well-heel'd subjects stoode,
To celebrate a quiet wedding-daye,
And eke affirm their faith in Nationhoode:
When times are ille, a touch of something goode,
Such as a knot in Royal marriage tied,
May serve to hide the knot that mars the woode.
Classes that cleave and Riches that divide
Fade in the loving union of a Groome and Bride.

24 July 1981

The SDP convert

Just for a gutful of Tony I left them,
Just for a last straw that stuck in my throat.
I, at the crossroads and come to a turning,
Thought it was time to be turning my coat.

We who have laboured so long in the vineyard,
Hoping to gather the fruits by-and-by,
Pin all our hopes on a wine that will warm us,
Now that the well of selection runs dry.

We shall march steadily, taking our chances,
Though they be slim and our principles small.
There will be more of us, boasting our purity,
Crossing our hands, lest our figleaves should fall!

9 October 1981

Goodbye, bobby

'I don't give a damn for the bleeding hearts, the
Marxist agitators and the so-called liberals.'
—Jim Jardine, chairman of the Police
Federation.

Now all that stands between us
And the leafless winter landscape,
Pitted with craters where dead things lie,
Is the conviction of being virtuous
And guardian of all that is best:
The time of pussyfooting is past
And Dixon has had his day.

The friendly nod and the shared joke
Have gone with the village bicycle
And the piece of pie from cook,
Along with that children's comic world.
Nothing can save us now but water,
Rubber bullets and the choking gas.

Perhaps we'll never have to use them:
Given luck, we may get by
With sprays to mark the individual
Agitator, the lone soft-hearted liberal;
Anything rather than identify the cause.
Anger allows no choice
To the rioter or the police;
We must love one another or dye.

17 July 1981

Tina and Titan

Tina—*'There is No Alternative.'*
(Tory slogan)
Titan—*'There Is Ted's*
Alternative Now.' (Another Tory
slogan)

Said Titan to Tina,
'I see the arena
Is crawling with victims
Who bleed from your cuts;
And would-be defectors,
Who fear the electors,
Are talking of garters
Made out of your guts.'

Said Tina to Titan,
'You can't hope to frighten
A lady in armour
Who follows her star.
To change in mid-season
By yielding to reason.
I'd have to be crazy.'
Said Titan, 'You are.'

And both, being caring
And loud in declaring
That mass unemployment
Was morally wrong,
Were true, in their fashion,
To one simple passion:
The weak to the wall,
And the loot to the strong.

16 October 1981

Norman's conquests

'The portents for the poor are ominous.'
—The Guardian, *on expenditure cuts to be announced by Norman Fowler, Social Services Secretary.*

'Tis the voice of the Fowler,
I heard him declare,
As he nervously clutched at
The straws in his hair:
'You can see from these figures
And glean from this chart
I've rejected soft options
To harden my heart.'

As a certified woodman
So he with his axe
Laid his hand to his task,
With his ears full of wax.
And his eyes brimmed with tears,
But his actions were bold
As he hacked at the helpless,
The sick and the old.

There were some who applauded
And others who wept,
While the rest made a rumbling
Noise as they slept.
And a handful revolted
By stirring their tea,
But not one was as half
As revolting as he.

23 October 1981

A loss for words

(After the Oxford Street bombing)

We need a new language now.
The old words stumble like dazed survivors
Through an aftermath of smoking wreckage,
And are no match for terror.

Nor are the customary speeches
Adequate to the final, sad salute,
To what is felt of pity and regard.
We cannot pay back what we owe.

Words do not insure against this loss.
A raging disbelief ties the innocent tongue,
And the breaking, eloquent voices
Fall silent before a joking courage.

Anger and fear, the coinage of our time,
Have been rubbed thin by daily usage,
Where nothing is gained but deeper wounds
And a bloodier hopelessness.

Useless to grope for the fitting phrase,
Or search for a despairing curse:
Nothing spells out what is deepest,
Beneath the mind's secret anxieties.

Mad and heartless is all we can say.
What words, then, for the crazed governors,
Builders of thousands of bombs,
Careful plotters of the death of millions?

30 October 1981

Please adjust your dress before grieving

Walter Johnson, Labour MP for Derby South, and other Members were 'disgusted' by Michael Foot's appearance at the Cenotaph Remembrance ceremony.

'He looked like an out-of-work navvy,'
The Member for Mumbleton said.
'His working-man's clothing,
Which filled me with loathing,
Is no way to honour the dead.

'A chap should remember his manners,
And have a blank space in his heart:
An absence of feeling
Is not unappealing,
As long as you're dressed for the part.'

So spoke the egregious Member,
Whose mind was incredibly small;
He knew private passion
Was hardly the fashion,
And public appearance was all.

Then up rose the voice of a soldier,
Who lay with a wound in his chest,
And said, as they mopped it,
'I wouldn't have copped it,
If I had been properly dressed.'

13 November 1981

Someone up there

*'Our intellectual and spiritual values are
rooted in the source of all strength, a
belief in a higher being, a law higher than
our own.'—President Reagan.*

Not for us the rule of iron,
Not for us the curtained lie;
We derive our deepest values
From our Sponsor in the sky.

We have pity for the Godless,
Servile in their total state;
Lenin made their land a prison,
Goodness made our country great.

We protect the huddled masses,
As we strive to serve the poor,
Bearing witness in Atlanta,
Sharing in El Salvador.

Kneeling to a higher being
Guards the simple things we love;
He who blesses our investments
Shines upon us from above.

You can always tell the good guys
By the holy hats they wear;
Someone up there who adores us
Sanctifies our ironware.

22 May 1981

Labour-rattling

'This election will provide the leaders of the party with an opportunity to show that they share the views of the members.'—Tony Benn.

How ghastly to hear Mr Benn
Coming out with such dangerous stuff!
As if the political fen
Weren't already stagnant enough!

His mind is alert and unsleeping,
His eyes are unnaturally bright;
His vigour is matchless in keeping
His pipe and his party alight.

His dream of a people's assembly
Is something we'd rather not see;
He has a deep passion for Wembley
And limitless gallons of tea.

He walks with a left inclination,
He looks to the top of the hill;
He plagues the elect of the nation,
And makes them exceedingly ill.

He ventures to raise certain issues
Best handled by sensible men,
And makes them weep into their tissues—
How awkward to face Mr Benn!

10 April 1981

No smoke without fire

A report in the Observer *suggests that pressure from the tobacco industry led to the shifting of anti-smoking Ministers from the Department of Health.*

Carcinoma of Imperium
By the nine brands he swore
That the great house of Player
Should suffer wrong no more.
By the nine brands he swore it,
And made a call that day,
And bade the Ministers pipe down,
Or else be blown away.

Then out spake Dr Gerard Vaughan,
The Minister of State:
'To every man upon this earth
Death cometh soon or late.
And how can man die better
Than with a furry tongue,
For the ash upon his waistcoat,
And the tumour on his lung?'

And all the good tobacco men
Could scarce forbear to cheer,
For they were free to advertise
By millions more a year.
And in return for benefits
Derived from sponsored sport,
A weak and last-gasp Government
Could count on their support.

20 November 1981

Frontline

And it will come again,
The phoenix fury rising from the ashes,
The raised arm after the raised profile
Even the blind foresaw.
And it will come again.

And it will come again
In other places and out of the same
Decay. There will be more than bricks
The next time, more than flame
And shattered glass and looted shop.
More than the gentle rain
Of missiles, more than the amatory
Clasp of hate and the indistinguishable
Blood.

And it will come again.
The unbelieving hand will be raised
In horror, the bewildered word
Will spew from microphone and press
And it will come again
From the picture-randy camera eye.
And nothing will be understood.

And it will come again.
The symptom will be solemnly recorded
As the disease. And most will forget
The red blood and the white law
And the bland unseeing blue.
And the black despair.

17 April 1981

Sexual Congress

The April issue of Playboy *reveals secret sexual practices among legislators in Washington.*

The lobbies are loud with the cries of the pleasured,
The toilets are crowded on Capitol Hill,
And using the yardstick by which they are measured,
Such acts are more urgent than blocking a bill.

Then hail to the Moral Majority,
Supporters of President Clean
And fitted to speak with authority
On matters that touch the obscene.

There's Congressman Bullshine, the pride of the nation,
A very close colleague of Senator Bray,
Who was quietly requested to take a vacation,
And later confessed to have had it away.

Then hail to our leaders who dreamingly,
While standing where Lincoln once trod,
Go down on their knees, although seemingly
Are not always praying to God.

13 March 1981

La belle dame sans raison

'There is something almost bizarre about the partnership between Mrs Thatcher, the Prime Minister, and her Secretary of State for Foreign Affairs (Lord Carrington).'—Ian Aitken in the Guardian.

O what can ail thee, cautious lord,
In doubt and plainly worrying?
Thy combination seems to lack
That certain thing.

I see a furrow in thy brow,
From which observers might construe
That thou hast not been taken in
By ballyhoo.

'I serve a Lady for my pains,
An unrepentant feudalist;
Her talk of guts would indicate
She's round the twist.

'I pointed to the map and said
She would inflame the Arab zone.
She looked at me and I could see
Her heart was stone.

'So rapid a deployment force
As she doth crave is hardly wise;
And that is why a yawning Gulf
Between us lies.

'I saw some death-pale statesmen too,
And they were climbing up the wall;
They cried—"La Belle Dame sans Raison
Will fix us all!"

'And this is why I mop my brow
In fear and vaguely wondering
What kind of long hot summer now
Will follow spring.'

6 March 1981

The Saviour

*'That government (in El Salvador) offers the
best hope of progress towards moderate
democracy.'—US Secretary of State
Alexander Haig.*

Amid the dark night that descends
On Latin American cities,
Dismaying our émigré friends
Who sit on outlandish committees,
Behold a bright beacon that gleams
And tells us Duarte is here—
El Salvador, bringer of dreams
And Saviour of all we hold dear.

We shall not stand idly by,
While towns are invested by terror;
The corpses that stare at the sky
Were probably murdered in error.
You cannot tame ravening beasts,
You need helicopters and guns
To pacify turbulent priests
And rout revolutionary nuns.

With Congress as tight as a clam,
Invasion is out of the question;
We don't want another Vietnam—
But thanks for your timely suggestion.
And if it is simply a case
Of driving the fiend from the door,
We shall not lack courage to face
The terrible threat of the poor.

27 February 1981

I Shall Vote Centre

(With apologies to Christopher Logue for updating his 'I Shall Vote Labour' of 1966)

I shall vote Centre because
the opinion-polls say I ought to vote Centre.
I shall vote Centre in order
to protect the sacred institution of *Any Questions*?
I shall vote Centre because the Centre has got it just about Right.
I shall vote Centre because I am fond of claret.
I shall vote Centre because Janet Suzman will vote Centre.
I shall vote Centre because
if I don't Benn will put me to work in the salt-mines.

AND

I shall vote Centre because
Shirley has been through a gruelling time.
I shall vote Centre because
my wife had her breasts fondled by a man on the Underground.
I shall vote Centre because
if I do not vote Centre I shall become impotent.
I shall vote Centre because I know how to pronounce Lech Walesa.
I shall vote Centre because my dentist is a member of CND.
I shall vote Centre because
I want to see the Fire Service handed back to private enterprise.
I shall vote Centre because there isn't enough sport on television.
I shall vote Centre because
I want to stop bus-conductors calling me 'squire'.
I shall vote Centre because
the Queen has a very difficult job and she does it superbly.
I shall vote Centre because, deep down,
I am very shallow.

13 February 1981

Chef's special

Mr James Prior, the Employment Secretary, aims to cut the unemployment figures by abolishing the compulsory registration of everyone out of work.

Oh, what is that smell
That floats from the kitchen
And seems like the scent
Of high pheasant on hooks?
Is it some sort of game
With a rarified name?
Is it fish? Is it meat?
No, it's simply a treat
Which the Chef has created
By cooking the books.

It could be a quarter
Or more of a million
Will vanish in bubbles
And billowing smoke.
What a brilliant device
To make paper taste nice,
So that figures we hate
To be served on a plate
Can be carved at the table
And cut at a stroke!

24 April 1981

Teacher knows best

*'Corporal punishment is most effective as part
of a positive and caring relationship between
teacher and pupil, as between parent and
child.'—the Assistant Masters Association.*

The punishment that children bear
In institutes of learning
Reflects their teachers' loving care
For strokes that soil their underwear
And keep the home fires burning.

Such practices are elsewhere banned,
But those are backward nations;
Assistant masters understand
There's nothing like a bleeding hand
For forging warm relations.

Though Captain Bligh, while all at sea,
Found what a harboured grudge meant,
The law of licensed tyranny
Demands that teachers should be free
To exercise their judgment.

Our caring floggers have a case,
Nor can their case be faulted:
They understand the modern child,
Who daily yearns to be defiled
And loves to be assaulted.

23 January 1981

Citation

When Mrs Thatcher visits the United States next month, she will receive the Donovan Award, established by veterans of the Office of Strategic Services, for rendering distinguished service in the interest of the democratic process and the cause of freedom.

She has served the cause of freedom,
She has raised the tyrant's yoke
From the shoulders of the humble
And the backs of decent folk,
Who are proud of being British,
And still more of being broke.

If the strong have cause to tremble
And the weak have cause to bless,
If the dawn of truth advances
And the shades of night regress,
It is thanks be to our Leader,
Not to say the O.S.S.

Let the joyful sirens greet her
Where the torch of freedom gleams,
Though receiving such a medal
Is more painful than it seems,
For it must be sheerest torture
Selling arms to some regimes.

16 January 1981

Jack the Lad

'All the dying want is a bit of T.L.C. (tender loving care).'—Squadron Leader Jack Curry, civil defence organiser at the Home Defence College, Easingwold.

'If ever the balloon goes up
And bits of flesh float down,
We'll still preserve an upper lip,'
Said Jack, the College clown.

'D-Day may seem a dim idea,
And war sound rather tame,
But vomiting and diarrhoea
Add interest to the game.'

'The living may be oozing pus,
And you can call me mad—
But that goes for the rest of us,'
Said laughing Jack the Lad.

'All the dying really want
Is a bit of TLC
And when their eyes begin to melt,
They'll look to chaps like me.'

The treatment when the blood turns black
Is tender loving care,
Though what is left of jolly Jack
Is neither here nor there.

9 January 1981

Glorious morning

'We looked at their philosophy, and they had a desire to make people understand what was happening.'—Lady Plowden, chairman of the IBA, on the franchise granted to TV-AM for breakfast television in 1983.

You must wake and call me early,
Call me early, mother dear,
In time to see the early show
(O that it were next year!).
Of all the treats in store, mother,
The maddest, merriest day
Will be when I get up at dawn
And yawn at Peter Jay!

Let us sing the hope of millions,
And the faith of Lady P
The happiest time for all mankind
Will be in '83,
When Rippon and Rantzen reign, mother,
And nobody counts the cost
Of the evergreen charm of Parkinson,
The vernal appeal of Frost!

What immensity of talent!
What a chance for thrusting youth,
With not a thought of private gain,
But a passion for public truth!
So here's to the early birds, mother,
And the worms who will understand
Why they knelt to the IBA, mother,
Who dealt them a lovely hand!

2 January 1981

On the side of the angels

The 6.4 per cent pay offer to nurses, which the Government refuses to improve, would leave a staff nurse with a salary of £90 a week.

O tiresome nurses, who merit our curses,
Greedy for more than you need or deserve,
Your lack of pity, which empties the kitty,
Makes Norman Fowler aghast at your nerve!
Instead of pressing for meat with your dressing,
Why can't you just be contented to serve?

A sense of mission, not naked ambition,
Surely should move Florence Nightingale's heirs;
She may inspire you, but who can admire you,
Claiming there's no other job that compares?
Apart from faeces, which have you in creases,
There's lifting stout patients from invalid chairs.

You say your wages have fallen for ages,
And life on a pittance is getting you down,
But look, come off it, you don't show a profit,
Nor can we dine off the blood on your gown.
You have no title, your job isn't vital,
Like stripping an asset or wearing a crown.

2 April 1982

The end of glory

We have ruled the seas for uncounted years
When the map was marked in red,
Though there's never a sage or a crystal ball
That can tell what lies ahead:
We have waved the flag in a hundred lands,
Where the heathen has feared John Bull.
If blood be the price of fantasy,
Lord God, we shall pay in full!

There's never a word from a foaming mouth
But speaks of a distant Brit;
There's never a sabre rattled now
But drops 'our lads' in the shit—
But sinks a fleet in the Commons bar
For the sake of our 'kith and kin'.
If blood be the price of 'unity',
Lord God, we shall pay it in!

We must gird our loins in a Union Jack,
And sail from a naval base,
And suffer the loss of a Carrington,
Which is better than losing face.
We must succour the Falkland Islanders,
And fight to their final breath.
If blood be the price of lunacy,
Lord God, we shall bleed to death!

9 April 1982

Discordant note

A proposal by four former US Government officials, notably ex-Defence Secretary Robert McNamara, that NATO should renounce the first use of nuclear weapons in Europe was publicly attacked by Secretary of State Alexander Haig before it was even published.

Offended by the raucous sound
Of McNamara's band,
The critic with the crystal mind
Condemns it out of hand.
If we forsake our sacred right
To blow the world away,
We may increase the threat to peace
We all enjoy today.

A doctrine loved by men of steel
And trained to play it tough
May look to those who pay the price
Like suicide or bluff;
But yielding a pre-emptive strike
Involves a larger risk:
Our trade in arms across the sea
Would not be half as brisk.

So let the eye be covered up
And deaf the ear we turn;
The lesson will be wasted breath,
If we refuse to learn.
It would be wrong to listen to
The pacifistic four:
They're only speaking for themselves—
And frantic millions more.

16 April 1982

All anti-fascists now

'Our people are under the heel of the Argentine invader.'
—Mrs Thatcher

In former times when certain crimes appeared in memoranda,
Our diplomats just raised their hats and called it propaganda.
It wasn't done to jump the gun, nor yet parade your passion,
And those who did, to free Madrid, were hardly in the fashion.
But now what harms the sale of arms to such as Galtieri
Is bloody war, which heretofore meant one more Bloody Mary.
When victims feel the tyrant's heel, our duty's to defend 'em;
If blown sky-high, they'll choose to die—and that by referendum.
The lady needs heroic deeds to prove that she is manly,
Which may require a world on fire and panic in Port Stanley.
A body-count is paramount, although a trifle skittish,
But pose the threat, lest we forget that they are almost British.
Thank God our press is more or less committed now to whoredom
And selling what is clearly hot and bound to banish boredom.
The time, no doubt, is running out, there may be repercussions;
We fight for God, but what a sod it's not against the Russians!

30 April 1982

St Margaret's Passion

'My passion is my country.'—Mrs Thatcher.

My passion is my country,
My country is my class;
My people raise their hands to praise
The scented wind I pass.

My ardour has no limit,
My longings have no end,
My thoughts imbue the lucky few
Who count me as a friend.

My fervour is unbounded
For individual choice;
The unemployed are overjoyed
To hear my soothing voice.

My love is for the humble,
Concern my sacred flame;
The railmen kneel to kiss my heel,
The nurses bless my name.

My will is made of iron,
My faith four inches thick,
My inner fire is my desire
To help the old and sick.

My passion is my country,
It rules my head and heart;
I weep for those who dare suppose
I do not give a fart.

15 January 1982

Good and faithful servant

'Joe Gormley may get some more tangible mark of the Government's gratitude in due course, to help ease the hard knocks he is getting from Arthur Scargill.'
—City Comment, Daily Telegraph.

Some of the lads have said 'Never!'
And some of the lads have said 'Yes',
And some have been guided, I reckon,
By reading the *Daily Express.*
I said what I thought of the ballot,
And told them to take it as Red;
Don't call it an act of betrayal,
Or I shall retire to my bed.

To undermine union decisions
Is tougher than digging for coal,
And those who are all for King Arthur
Should listen to President Mole.
And when I hand over in April,
Declaring my conscience is clear,
I'll live out my days on a pension,
And shrink from becoming a peer.

Whenever the Board made an offer,
I always considered their case.
(I learnt how to crawl on my stomach
When doing a stint at the face).
Whatever I did as a leader,
I did with no thought of reward,
And I'll be as stunned as the next man
If ever they make me a Lord.

22 January 1982

Skivers and railwaymen

Newspapers in Rupert Murdoch's News Group have been blacked by train drivers because of a Sun article alleging fiddling by ASLEF members.

In critical times,
When the bank-rate climbs and falls,
The citizen, to ease his stress,
May turn towards the dunghill press.
If the kind of news
That he may peruse appals,
He'll not for long remain impassive,
Having seen it as a massive load of balls—
Though Rupert's tune is that he would sooner die
Than peddle in dirt or ever print a lie.

Skivers and railwaymen,
Are news in the midden Sun.
What makes the clearest sense is
To fiddle one's expenses,
But fixing a sheet in Bouverie Street
Is seldom, if ever, done,
And what is least amusing
Is boozing.
When they go to lunch,
What they love to munch
Is a lettuce-leaf with chives.
When there's work to do,
They are back by two,
And never betray their wives
At News Group
Their spirits droop
When somebody rapes a nun,
But skivers and railwaymen
Are news in the midden Sun.

29 January 1982

Doctor on the game

*According to the Association of Scientific,
Technical and Managerial Staffs, some medical
consultants are getting their private patients
treated in NHS hospitals and charging
them fees.*

When I was a medical student,
I lived in a prostitute's flat.
I thought, when she told me her takings,
That I could do better than that.
And once having learnt of the hazards
Of such a precarious trade,
I vowed to become a consultant,
A sure way of getting it made.

Hippocrates laid down the ethics,
But I'm no impractical Greek:
His oath, which is solemn and binding,
I took with my tongue in my cheek.
The code of your ideal physician
Precludes the amassing of wealth,
But as I keep telling my conscience,
I'm not in this job for my health.

The list of my qualifications
Is there on my Harley Street plate,
Which gives me a licence to follow
The practice of milking the State.
I smile when I hear people talking
And arguing over the wine:
Whatever they say about whoring,
The oldest profession is mine.

19 February 1982

Right-hand Foot

I saw an aged, aged man,
   A-sitting in a trench.
'How do you serve, Sir?' I began,
   'The Opposition bench?'
He said, 'By treading on the dream
   Of what I was before,
And sacking members of my team,
   Who vote against the war.'

Now if in mind I should be put
   To dye my whiskers blue,
Or madly squeeze a right-hand foot
   Into a left-hand shoe,
Or if I drop upon my toe
   A very heavy wrench,
I weep, for it reminds me so
Of that old man I used to know—
Whose look was wild, whose gait was slow,
Whose hair was whiter than the snow,
Whose voice was like a sudden blow,
With eyes like cinders, all aglow,
Who seemed to know which way to go,
Whose speech now waffles to and fro,
And mutters ramblingly and low,
As if his mouth were full of dough,
Who snorted like a buffalo—
In Ebbw Vale, so long ago,
   A-sitting on a bench.

28 May 1982

Epitaph on a team of mercenaries

(After A.E. Housman)
*'There is no meeting point at all between those
who want to play cricket and those who want a
revolution in South Africa.'*—Daily Telegraph.

These, in the cause of bat-and-balling,
When others took the rules as read,
Followed their mercenary calling
And took their Kruggerrands instead.

Their passion and their purses blended;
They heard the cries and turned away;
What most rejected, these defended,
And closed their eyes to earn their pay.

5 March 1982

Damned spots

*'For Mr Foot and his colleagues to pick first on
Mr Tatchell and then on Mr Wall is like
scratching at single spots on a body
festooned with pimples.'*—Daily Telegraph.

How doth the Daily Telegraph
Improve its graceful style,
And add to every mirthless laugh
A bucketful of bile!

How stirring is its voice, how bold,
How bravely it goes forth,
And makes its readers' blood run cold
With news from Bradford North!

A bright and healthy flush it sees
As spots upon the skin,
Dread symptom of some foul disease
That might be voted in.

And while these blemishes and sores
On parties named and known
May turn its stomach, it ignores
The pustules on its own.

12 March 1982

So long

'So long as an Adam and Eve survived in every little hamlet and so long as they liked each other, we shall have this nation going on again.'
—*Wing Commander P. Harle, head of civil defence in Hampshire.*

So long as Adam and his mate
Still have the strength to copulate,
This nation, after such a war,
Will be in business as before.

So long as they, though deaf and blind,
Can reproduce the human kind,
So long will Eve upon her back
Give birth beneath the Union Jack.

She may have radioactive eggs
And he be short of arms and legs,
But just as long as they can fuck,
We'll still get by, with any luck.

Their flesh might burn, their ears might bleed,
There might be mutants from his seed,
But nature, when the world has gone,
Will keep this nation going on.

Their fruitful life, of course, depends
On being more than just good friends,
And able still to recognise
The fondness in their melted eyes.

So long as there's a loving-cup
To keep their British spirits up,
And neither of them is insane,
This nation will go on again.

26 March 1982

Half a loaf

'Some elections are better than no elections.'
—Eldon Griffiths, Conservative MP, one of the
Parliamentary team visiting El Salvador.

Can't run before you learn to crawl,
Half a loaf's better than none at all.
Mouldy it may be and chewed by rats
In shiny boots and braided hats,
But given the facts, you can't want more
From the hard-pressed chaps in El Salvador.

Nobody registered? Well, that's true.
Dead in the ditches? A few, a few.
Justice is swift and a trifle stern,
As those who oppose are quick to learn,
But given the needs of a bloody war,
They're doing things right in El Salvador.

You say it's rigged? Don't make me tired,
A sense of proportion is what's required.
I'd say the chances were pretty fair
Of practically free elections there,
And I'm more convinced than ever before
Of the right result in El Salvador.

19 March 1982